Models, Strategies, and Methods for Effective Teaching

Models, Strategies, and Methods for Effective Teaching

Hellmut R. Lang
University of Regina, Emeritus

David N. Evans
University of Regina

PEARSON

Boston • New York • San Francisco
Mexico City • Montreal • Toronto • London • Madrid • Munich • Paris
Hong Kong • Singapore • Tokyo • Cape Town • Sydney

Executive Editor and Publisher: *Stephen D. Dragin*
Series Editorial Assistant: *Meaghan Minnick*
Marketing Manager: *Tara Kelly*
Editorial Production Service: *Omegatype Typography, Inc.*
Composition and Manufacturing Buyer: *Andrew Turso*
Electronic Composition: *Omegatype Typography, Inc.*
Photo Researcher: *Omegatype Typography, Inc.*
Cover Administrator: *Joel Gendron*

For related titles and support materials, visit our online catalog at www.ablongman.com.

Between the time website information is gathered and then published, it is not unusual for some sites to have closed. Also, the transcription of URLs can result in typographical errors. The publisher would appreciate notification where these errors occur so that they may be corrected in subsequent editions.

Library of Congress Cataloging-in-Publication Data

Lang, Hellmut R.
  Models, strategies, and methods for effective teaching / Hellmut R. Lang, David N. Evans.—1st ed.
    p. cm.
  Includes bibliographical references and index.
  ISBN 0-205-40841-9
    1. Teachers—Training of—United States. 2. Effective teaching—United States. I. Evans, David N. II. Title.

LB1715.L24 2006
370'.71'1—dc22

2005048918

Printed in the United States of America

10 9 8 7 6 5 4   10 09

Photo credits: p. 1, copyright © Michael Newman/PhotoEdit; p. 163, copyright © Bill Aron/PhotoEdit; p. 335, copyright © David Young Wolff/PhotoEdit. All rights reserved.

Contents

Preface

Models, Strategies, and Methods for Effective Teaching has been written to respond to the challenges to teacher education presented by national and state legislation and the frustrations expressed by teacher education graduates who found it difficult to transfer what was studied on campus to the reality of modern schools and classrooms. This book was written to help you whether you are a teacher education student or practicing professional.

There is significant research-based information on what makes an effective teacher. For example, Danielson (1996) has identified the essential components that teachers need to master to promote improved student learning. Her framework provides a road map for novice teachers, guidance for professional excellence, and a structure for focusing improvement efforts and communication with the larger community. Teachers can have a clear idea of what they need to know and do to be effective and how to help the public understand what teachers do.

In the United States there are several sources of guidelines for the teacher in the new millennium. These include the Professional Assessments for Beginning Teachers (PRAXIS) series, the Interstate New Teacher Assessment and Support Consortium (IN-TASC), and the National Board for Professional Teaching Standards (NBPTS), which sets standards for teachers. Universities and colleges also have guidelines to help the novice teacher become a successful educator.

In this text we present a pre-service and in-service model, the Teacher Competence Profile (TCP). The TCP is built on the Intern Professional Profile (IPP) developed by Art McBeath, Hellmut Lang, and others at the University of Regina, Saskatchewan, Canada, in collaboration with school system personnel. It has been used successfully since the 1980s and continues to be used for pre-service and in-service professional development by the University of Regina and school districts. The set of descriptors for each competency (designed by Hellmut Lang and David Friesen) is particularly useful. We have modified and added to the IPP descriptors to provide an up-to-date set of competencies and descriptors. It is these descriptors, based on research, that take the profile a step beyond the Danielson rubric. Although it can be used as an assessment tool, the TCP is a valuable profile and functional source of competencies for teacher professional development.

The research is there. We know what needs to be achieved and how to develop effective knowledge, skills, and practices. More and more teacher training programs reflect a constructivist approach through which the novice teacher can build success through a blend of theory and practice. As McLeskey and Waldron (2004) observe,

> Knowledge for practice is perhaps the most widely accepted perspective on teacher learning. . . . This perspective holds that the more teachers know about subject matter, instructional strategies, effective interventions, and so forth, the more effectively they will teach. . . . [The] new image of teacher learning and related professional development has moved to a more constructivist model of instruction, and away from a transmission model. (pp. 5–6)

Another potentially positive development in the United States is the No Child Left Behind (NCLB) Act of January 8, 2002. This is so even though, as reported by Dobbs (2005) in the *Washington Post,* teachers' unions and some state legislatures have depicted the law as an underfunded federal mandate, overly cumbersome and bureaucratic. The four pillars of NCLB are (1) accountability and testing, (2) flexibility and local control, (3) funding for what works, and (4) expanded parental options. It replaces the federal Elementary and Secondary Education Act (ESEA) of 1965 and is the principal federal law affecting K–12 education in the United States today. President Bush pronounced, "Today begins a new era, a new time for public education in our country. Our schools will have higher expectations—we believe every child can learn. From this day forward, all students will have a better chance to learn, to excel, and to live out their dreams." These are high ideals, and the act has already had profound positive and negative effects on schooling.

Teacher preparation is at a crossroads. On one hand, the potential for excellence has never been better, with so many approaches to teaching possible; on the other hand, teachers and teacher educators are faced with state-imposed requirements and trends that threaten to reduce the act of teaching to transmission of knowledge in order to meet the pressures of standardized test requirements.

There is a danger that national and state standards will be used, not to guide and enhance teacher education and practice, but to force teachers to follow a rigid formula that contravenes their beliefs of what students need and deserve. There is a danger that the NCLB movement will lead to teachers drilling students for success, mainly in language arts and mathematics, to the neglect of other parts of a well-rounded curriculum. School districts may respond to the call for accountability by overusing or misusing standardized tests to meet the required standards.

Thorough, high-quality teacher education is critical. A 2004 education symposium to discuss teacher quality was hosted by the James B. Hunt, Jr., Institute, with governors, state education advisors, and experts in attendance. The conclusion was that college graduates with education degrees are unprepared for the rigors of the classroom, especially in schools with large numbers of poor, minority, and special needs students; and that too many teachers wash out of the profession each year as a result of inadequate preparation. Schools of education, particularly at public universities, have failed to provide the training needed to prepare teachers. This issue has gained urgency because of NCLB, which will require all classroom teachers to have bachelor's degrees, pass state subject and pedagogy tests, and be fully certified in their state by 2006. Therefore, it is critical that colleges and universities prepare students well.

We believe that the means to address the positive and negative concerns is provided through this text. The framework is the Teacher Competence Profile. Chapter by chapter, the essential knowledge and skills for effective teaching are presented. Each chapter contains recent research and good practice with respect to the theme discussed. This is followed by guidelines for the teacher, and, finally, practical approaches are presented. For example, in Chapter 6, on classroom management, the current and classic scholarship on classroom management are presented first; then specific guidelines and suggestions for effective practice are explored; followed by examples, cases, and activities. Novice teachers can use case studies, activities, microteaching, and school classrooms to construct personal meaning and develop teaching skills.

We are aware that "new" is not always better. Over the years, educators, psychologists, philosophers, and others have made major contributions to teaching research. People such as Piaget, Dewey, Vygotsky, Bloom, Maslow, and Kounin have added to the knowledge base of teachers. We have endeavored to build on these contributions.

Finally, we recognize that theory grows out of practice and practice informs theory— the relationship is symbiotic. We suggest ways in which novice teachers can use action research to contribute to teacher education knowledge and practice. For example, teachers can consider the question, "Will more higher-level questions enhance the learning of my students?" Teachers can follow the guidelines in this text as the basis for investigation and arrive at their own research results.

This text, with its professional development TCP model, can guide you to best practice. Congratulations in having chosen one of the world's great professions!

Acknowledgments

The inspiration for *Models, Strategies, and Methods for Effective Teaching* has been years of partnerships with the stakeholders in teacher education in Saskatchewan, Canada. Teacher education programs that collaborated and piloted the model and content were the Faculty of Education, University of Regina; the Saskatchewan Urban Native Teacher Education Program (SUNTEP) Gabriel Dumont Institute; and the Teacher Education Department, First Nations University of Canada (FNUC). Saskatchewan cooperating teachers and administrators have provided valuable feedback. Special thanks go to the many teacher education students for their involvement and ideas. Other important collaborators have been the Regina Public and Separate School Systems, the Saskatchewan Department of Education, and the Saskatchewan School Trustees Association.

The Saskatchewan Urban Native Teacher Education Program (Regina) deserves much credit for this book. It provides teacher education for Métis and Indian students, and offers an outstanding teacher education program that was a major inspiration for this text. Hellmut Lang helped design the program and taught in it for over twenty years.

The dedication, drive, and innovativeness of Art McBeath have had a major impact on the creation of this text. Valuable input has been received from Errol Young, Cyril Kesten, Donna Scarfe, Sandra Blenkinsop, George Richert, Ray Petracek, Larry Lang, David Friesen, and Fred Bessai.

We would like to thank the following reviewers for their comments on this manuscript: Louise D. Baucom, University of North Carolina at Charlotte; Robert H. Fowler, University of Victoria; William Michael Hessmiller, II, CET Editors and Training Associates; Melba Spooner, University of North Carolina at Charlotte; and M. Thomas Worley, Armstrong Atlantic State University.

H. R. L.
D. N. E.